The Silent Epiphany

How mediocre and primary the world looks through our sights, yet how beautifully extraordinary it seems when we gaze at it

Akkriti Tiwari

INDIA • SINGAPORE • MALAYSIA

Copyright © Akkriti Tiwari 2023
All Rights Reserved.

ISBN 979-8-89067-805-8

This book has been published with all efforts taken to make the material error-free after the consent of the author. However, the author and the publisher do not assume and hereby disclaim any liability to any party for any loss, damage, or disruption caused by errors or omissions, whether such errors or omissions result from negligence, accident, or any other cause.

While every effort has been made to avoid any mistake or omission, this publication is being sold on the condition and understanding that neither the author nor the publishers or printers would be liable in any manner to any person by reason of any mistake or omission in this publication or for any action taken or omitted to be taken or advice rendered or accepted on the basis of this work. For any defect in printing or binding the publishers will be liable only to replace the defective copy by another copy of this work then available.

Contents

Part I: Ethereal.

Part II: Affection.

Part III: The Truth.

Preface

I have never regarded myself as a person who thinks unconventionally, at the risk of being modest, as someone who thinks differently.

I present to you my second poetry book after "wanderlust of words", the silent epiphany. For as long as I can remember, I have been imagining so many small elements in life in such a peculiar manner, and I believe that is the key to writing poetry that makes one imagine beyond the bonds of mediocrity. It is letting go of the wooden frame that is on the window to imagination, the roof which covers the house when the sky is nothing but a void of imagination, it is when you choose to free your thoughts and see things as more than what they are. This book is a collection of about 60 poems and write ups (rounded off) and contain probably the most bizarre yet, beautiful thoughts i have ever had. An epiphany is a very deep realisation of something, in abstract profundity. And all these realisations and thoughts that I had silently in my mind have been compiled into this book. The greatest compliment a writer can have, as per me, is that as a reader, a person could imagine whatever they were thinking of with utmost perfection, and in most of my poems, I have tried to achieve that. But, at the same time, I will not undermine the purity of the reader's imagination and their differing perceptions on one singular writing, in fact, it would give me the utmost feeling of pride if my readers imagine what I have written in more than one way. The book is divided into three spectrums, "ethereal" where I have mostly connected one thing to another and built up a passage of words between describing them and finding one common ground, though there is not much primary difference in the writings, as they mostly end up speaking about the universe philosophically, however, it's the topics I believe will interest you the most.

"Affection" is about love, and grief, and emotions altogether described in metaphorical ways, as a young writer.

And lastly, "the truth" truths about our society, about how things work that will leave a question in your mind, with write ups about mental health and perfectionism.

I guess that one thing is similar in all of the poems and write ups, fundamentally, and that is they are very metaphorically put together, and I hope that intrigues you too.

Lastly, i want to mention my family for their endless encouragement and faith in me,

Thank you.

Acknowledgement

I would like to express my deepest appreciation to my parents and my school, Sir Padampat Singhania Education Centre, Kanpur. My school has provided me with a fellowship under the scheme of Smt. Manorama Govind Hari Singhania Fellowship for Aspiring Authors.

My heartfelt gratitude to the School Management and the Principal, Ms. Bhawna Gupta, their motivation has made this journey special for me.

I would also like to mention my family as, without their presence that brought out the best in me, their incandescent light of affection which gave me the most beautiful thoughts, and their support, I wouldn't have been able to write this book as wonderfully as I did.

Thank you.

Part I

Ethereal.

1

Blurry, Yet Beautiful.

Things that seem so blurry sometimes appear so beautiful as well because when it's freezing outside and you're sitting inside the car,

The window next to you is covered with fog, just another winter evening, is it though?

I mean you get to draw blurry hearts with your fingers, although, you don't care which surroundings the car will pass by, the people either, It's just a heart, how does it even matter?

You'll never accept it but it does,

The mist makes the perfect canvas, and the delicacy and detail don't go that unnoticed now, do they? The way your mind lets your fingers touch the cold tempered glass without thinking twice, almost too intrigued by it, even though your hands are the coldest they have ever been because there's no one whose palms can warm them up. You still choose to draw that mellow little heart so casually but is it that casual? The arch of your index finger is so peculiar, it tells me otherwise. *It reminds you there's still hope,* Even if it's simply a heart on a window, so simple it looks like a child's colouring except finally there's no one to dictate

"You have to paint in between the lines"

That's what gives you the feeling of being boundless, that's the hope you fondle so gently. You simply poured your soul out when you drew on that paradise of a window, reminding yourself of its fragility, the admiration it deserves, the words it is worthy of hearing.

"I'll always believe in you."

You're worried about your little sketch fading away by the end of the ride,

But I promise you, it won't.

2

Profundity in a Canvas.

Art, art is everywhere they say,

Yet all they imagine is a piece of paper and paints.

Insanity or profundity,

it may be called whatsoever,

But I believe

Canvas is subtle in our eyes,

And we paint it with art every time we speculate,

Each time we perceive,

While others click pictures of the impeccably beautiful sky,

I am fascinated by the amount of composition God has painted it with,

From blue to pink to violet,

the colours dance in it like it's a kaleidoscope of pleasure and despair and love and hatred,

Acne reminds me of fragile roses,

Yet to flourish and prosper and thrive and grow,

In that vulnerable age where even seconds seem like days if not hours, *charm and grace are just so generous to cultivate in you.*

Our bodies are canvases,

the most modern masterpieces,

And carry the oldest of refinement that God made.

Deep blue eyes look like the ocean chose to reside in us,

Whereas brown look like the mountains did.

Our brains erupt with synapses between neurons every single day,

That look like galaxies and thunders,

Charisma and magnificence.

In the end, we are made of the same heavens as the stars,

In the same galaxy as the sun,

I wonder and ponder,

About all these pretty elements,

Lying right within us,

We don't see or hear,

But the power of the beyond,

Continues to cradle.

3

The Language of Flowers.

A vivid imagination, yet a peculiar sight.

It was a nuance that I witnessed,

Perhaps her breaths sounded like the blossoming of a flower,

and her eyelids were like golden butterflies,

and she curled and bent and twisted and turned into a chrysanthemum as she slept so precious and deep.

And quite a lot like people called her,

she was an exotic rose,

A lover of spirit, *she would visit the stars as soon as her eyes closed.*

But I had grown to believe she turned into a new flower each day when she slept,

on the days she felt lucky to be alive she turned into a water lily or the days she felt fury, a rose, with spikes all over her body, head to toe.

It could be the sign of the moonlight or the incremental shifting of the clouds,

the universe astounded her and power had aroused,

she turned into a flower every time she slept,

and science had left with all due respect.

I would argue every day with the people that I met,

"She is a flower"

but everyone laughed and wept,

how hilarious I was, talking about a person being a flower,

but the enigma that she carried was unmistakable,

and sometimes the nights she didn't sleep too well,

left petals in the strands of her hair and cutin on her skin but she still hid perfectly well under plain sight, as if nobody witnessed this part of her life.

Flowers do ignite,

and I was expecting one day she would too but maybe god had gifted her this freedom of living between space and time as soon as she closed her eyes,

only because he saw that her heart was blooming crystallised daisies,

and she had creepers and climbers instead of rib cages,

The lines in the palms of her hands too were stranded into the veins of leaves,

I couldn't differentiate after a point.

I knew her uniqueness, fascinated by her identity.

But I still wondered,

how could the others not see?

The way roots shaped each inch of her brown hair,

her eyes melancholy,

she was a masterpiece,

an abstract cration, artistic articulation.

Maybe the others couldn't see but I could, because I, I was potentially one of her kind.

4

To Break the Barriers, to Reach the Stars.

When I was younger, I would practise drawing stars in as many ways as I could, a triangle overlapped by another, it was quite simple, but I looked for ways I could make it complicated since it was my greatest wish while being 13 that I wanted my signature to include a star. And that obsession was due to an exceptionally superficial fact I had learnt,

"At the most fundamental level, we are very identical to the stars"

The definition of the universe for me at that very young age, fortunately, was that I was the descendant of such enigma, "the unknown"

that the other world we observe in the sky is in fact linked to our very own.

As I grew older, I realised that the universe is not just those infinitesimal dots, it is in fact many diverse worlds haphazardly jotted down together like it were all a coincidence, though that was only partially accurate.

At first in fact, when scientists were convinced that the universe was static, per them, stars had no motion or direction in the universe, they existed being stuck, embedded in the space-time sheet like meticulously formulated puzzle pieces, there were many hypotheses that supported this theory until later they discovered that all the stars that we could and eventually couldn't observe were drifting away from each other and from us through the spectra of light that they radiated till our very own minuscule world in this immensity of nothingness.

It was also eventually known that stars ultimately collapse into themselves due to their own gravity, that they are nothing but almost ever-lasting magnificent light bulbs that will someday run out of fuel.

Would the night sky still gleam for me knowing someplace in the cosmos at every millisecond perishing, a star in the universe just lost its shine?

Yet, on the contrary, I find it so intriguing how practically, unaffectedly such occurrences take place at such a tremendous distance from us, but at the same time, the field of physics is so captivating and generates curiosity beyond the realm of practicality that it caused Galileo to turn his telescope towards the sun and discover black spots on it which *unknowingly caused his own blindness.* That was the pain he suffered from falling in love with stars so greatly.

A black hole is a star too engulfed in itself, it contains so much gravity within itself that it does not permit light to escape.

Imagine being so dense, so mystically majestic that nothing can ever escape from you. A black void of nothingness in space.

Not words, not emotions, not even radiance or rays of the glow of identity,

Not even light.

From the books I have read, black holes have been an incredible mystery to unravel for scientists, yet, it's not the mystery that mesmerises me, it is the empathy I have built for them. For having so much affinity inside of them that even light cannot escape, they aren't so black at all now, are they?

They say beauty is often isolated, but a black hole isolates its very own being.

They say scientists are often a little mad, but I have grown to believe they fall in love with the beyond, *beyond the simple means of our comprehension.*

5

A Child's Painting.

Drips of Yellow, splatters of red and a smudge of green.

A fingerprint of blue and no, the lines were not coordinated enough to perfectly create the face of a person from the graphite pencil tip, in fact, they were hardly even sharpened.

Smudged.

It was a child's painting, one with no real sense or real meaning.

But I refuse to believe that,

Chaos is *mesmerising*, chaos is *hope*, chaos brings serenity at a level *beyond human perception*,

The universe is chaos.

So was the painting, which made me question if maybe the universe did indeed hide in those tiny artefacts that go unnoticed yet consist of the most glorious heavens and the most exuberant stars.

If there is some hidden uniqueness, if the patterns of the sky match those drops of paint splattered on the page, if perhaps, *the most chaotic stories are the closest to oblivion.*

6

Marvels.

Refinery reached its epitome when the light rays travelled and diversified through the drop of rain,

And when I peeked at what I could see through a wine glass,

my eyes shifted from the fragile crystal equation to his handsomely young eyes,

I found serenity, a sense of euphoria fled through my veins to my heart and my lungs, and *I found breath.*

I wonder if the sun rays too found their breath when they formed a rainbow,

They celebrated achieving the ultimate purpose in their short life span, a perplexing yet simply decadent vision of colours banded together like they'd be linked and belonged for the time they existed in our world.

"They were each other's breath".

Maybe if the wine glass had specks of minor inconveniences,

It wouldn't have been able to form his eyes so perfectly exquisite, complexion with such complexity the word "simple" had to be used.

Maybe if the raindrop fell faster than the light travelled, I, no, we all would've lost sight of the phenomenon of a rainbow, the lights would be lost, their purpose and soulfulness would've fallen under a puddle of the same raindrops and died and birthed dullness.

I fell and felt and tried to forget about minor inconveniences, but what would've happened to me if I never saw him that day I was admiring a wine glass like it was all I could do and then I admired his dove eyes, eyes that had *a sparkle which invited my everything, that sparkle I realised, was something worth rebelling for.*

my curiosity and fate joined hands, I met him.

if I didn't see a rainbow that day I was at my lowest, the day I needed light and light could swivel into breath, *breaths of a diminutive satisfaction that could ultimately overpower my grief.*

Yes, things in the world that are considered marvels too have their times and to get that promotion, I needed to wait for mine.

I shuddered to imagine.

Before I could realise the words poured out of me

"I think I'm in love"

And I still wonder if I meant to say that to the divinity or him.

7

Abstract Perfection.

Perfection has always meant systematic intricacy,

But it doesn't create a meticulous legacy,

The legacy of abstraction.

Enchanted by the universe,

I find it in our eyes,

How the colours dance in them like in the nebulae,

from brown to blue, to green, a tint of violet,

There are ripples of perplexing hypotheses, of those very few colours,

Yet to be deciphered, because there is no scientific testimony on how something so beyond magnificent even resembles something so, well, normal.

And when I accidentally caught a glimpse of my dog's eyes,

I drowned staring so profoundly into their refinement, As if *I found a way to travel through the heavens.*

I looked up at the night sky, to find answers,

But all I was left with was even more confusion,

How did the stars manage to create the same pattern,

As the freckles on my friend's skin?

And I felt delighted that we carry the stars in our skins without a speck of realisation.

So complex, I said, but how remarkable is this,

And yet, the wonder remained unsettled in my mind,

How the veins of our blood corresponded to the alignment of Rivers I saw from the window seat of the plane I was at,

Blood or water,

I could no longer make a difference,

Maybe because in the end,

They both carried the potion of survival.

The curiosity in my mind still doesn't settle,

But it is not my place to question a "why",

It Is just a glimpse of the power of the almighty.

Philosophical lenses possess it,

Chaos, maybe mayhem,

There are so many words to describe it,

"Abstraction"

And I ponder if that legacy is even remotely sane.

8

The Upside Down Reality.

I didn't run away

But did my feet just tiptoe to the middle of nowhere?

Pebbles upfront arranged in a peculiar manner till what looked to me as infinity,

I did not know the road I stood upon,

But I assumed it was life.

And the streams of the river were everywhere beside and around me,

I could see the world from an aeroplane in the sky,

The upside-down reality.

But there I told cluelessly with pebbles and pebbles in front of me,

Some were fading and hard,

Looked as if, if I stepped on them, I would tear my foot apart.

And others were soft as a cushion, waiting for me to step on them,

Tip, top, tip, top, the water fell slowly and gently,

And suddenly I felt a timid feeling far away in my heart,

What if I trip?

I would fall into obliviousness and lose it all,

I would fall into the scenic beauty of an aeroplane.

It wasn't scary, there was a certain allure to that thought,

To explore infinity,

Maybe those pebbles were keeping me hold,

From falling in too deep,

But maybe for me, the way of living had always been falling

The risk of attaining too much knowledge, too much of something,

Maybe falling made me feel like flying.

But I stood still,

Tip, toe, tip, toe.

I looked up at the world, the world of mine,

And then at the pebbles so peculiarly and intricately arranged it almost suffocated me.

"The sound gradually stopped, She fell."

9

A Room with No Voice.

Have you ever heard what a room with no voice sounds like?

When even walking down steps sounds like whispers that crawl down your ears,

Trickling their way through your skin,

carving fortresses of footprints as they travel through your body,

And writing with a pen sounds so amplified,

it feels as if the same pen had written the greatest of myths and stories,

Scraping its way through the letters of your heart and mine.

Curving its own body to form the neurons of our minds,

It certainly didn't seem to witness wonders, it created them.

The rustling of the pages,

sound like the shifting and swaying of leaves on an autumn evening,

Wind caressing and fondling them roughly and timidly,

Like a child does his mother when hungry.

And if you hear close enough,

You can hear your own tingling breaths,

as you inhale it feels like the world caves in,

The sense of reality whooshes with the air inside of you, and even if for a millisecond it feels like living inside the white screen of a broken computer,

Or in the silent, cold white light of a refrigerator,

Somewhat peaceful, serene.

But when you exhale,

Everything goes away the same way it came inside of you, the world entirely caves out, the reality sets itself in,

Maybe that is why we sigh in happy situations,

In sad ones too we attempt to exhale the pain with reality.

As you incline closer, you can hear a pattern in these voices,

The clock chimes twice, and her paws make a noise like raindrops on a summer night, and the rustles of the pages give it all a balance and the way the pen falls to the ground sounds exactly like a tree falling in a storm, and the way I breathe, sounds like your words when you speak,

"Da bum, da bum, da bum", that's the voice where all of them converge,

I might conceivably be delusional, but,

My heartbeat sounded just like that.

10

Aimlessness.

Your skin was pure white,

white as marbles and snow,

and freshly cooked rice even,

But as your beauty deserved it,

your attire wasn't designer or luxurious,

The shirt you wore was ripped from the arms,

And as if they were clawed with dust,

Your bare knees were visible from your pants,

I doubted if You had eaten anything since the morning,

Were you even wearing shoes?

But you had an axe in your hands,

You were a worker, a beautiful one,

A worker walking into the most massive,

And majestic and glorious building I had to lay my eyes upon,

About nearly as magnificent as how angelic your hands looked,

It looked as if someone had sculpted glass in the form of human skin,

I could only see your back as I walked across you,

and your itty bitty tired steps in the burning warmth,

Maybe your feet quivered in fear of the demonic heat that overpowered the ground underneath, but did that demon even matter?

I saw you as if you were walking aimlessly into that building,

As if you did not have hopes about what was to come,

Were the clutches of slavery tightening just a little bit too much?

The Gulmohar tree that shades my house,

It too seemed aimless to me today morning,

Like its branches extended towards the blue skyline,

In hopes to find out what's in the beyond,

To reach its sole master,

It was climbing ladders of the air, trying to resist the force of gravity just a little bit maybe,

And simultaneously it found joy on its way towards it,

Like the butterfly which sat on its leaves, leaves so broad as though they may be symbolised your thoughts, and she, she found a part of her in your thoughts so she sat on it,

You liked it because she gave you nurture on your way,

God was so beautiful once again because I hope you realise someday that he was inside the butterfly, present there as he saw your determination, present in your journey,

Maybe all the trees I've ever seen in my life,

They have the same purpose,

to see who reaches the sky first,

To see who touches the heavens first,

But I doubt there's ever any rivalry,

You see that's the difference between humans and trees,

We too have a purpose in life, but we do not have the bond of harmony,

Maybe that is why our wings of unity turn into clutches of slavery before even being born,

Were you being called by your master too?

Just as the angel of a worker was being called into slavery,

There is an entire difference between you two,

But you both were aimless,

wandering at the end,

Wandering as my thoughts,

My thoughts too float around my mind,

In hopes to touch the sky,

the sky at the end of philosophy and knowledge,

Because they say that when you are a poet,

You write till you bleed,

But I end up writing till that bled blood dries up.

Maybe that is aimless poetry.

Sometimes I tend to imagine our aimlessness has diamonds and emeralds embedded in it,

And it might be the reason that your branches haven't touched the sky yet,

Because the crowns of your beauty carry the depth of peace in them,

And so you touched the sky before even beginning your journey,

It might be that your marble white skin carries too many marbles,

In this world, it's become blinding to people,

Those who sit at the top of capitalist hierarchy,

And it might be that my aimless philosophy has just found its wings,

It might be that my aimless philosophy,

It's meant to be aimless.

11

I Saw Right Through Your Heart.

I saw right through your heart, you hid it from me. You told me all that you held captive inside that chest of yours was an organ working day and night to help you live since the moment you took birth, you told me it was the size of your fist, you told me it was just your heart, just so ordinary? I saw right past that.

I realised your heart is more of a well, sculpted by a sculptor so unique they're found in fairy tales, found in the snowy hills when the hikers run short of breath, in the tree that sheds its leaves even in springtime, and they managed to mould that well with so much love it almost has a fountain of affection built in it.

You told me your heart is just another heart, you didn't tell me it was a world of its own?

You didn't tell me that well was a passage to wonderland, a wonderland with magical amenities and extravagances, but with more orchids of condolences than roses of love,

a wonderland which was a glitch into the depths of the universe,

you have a heart that could make me believe the world is nothing but a simulation.

A wonderland with such brief notations, brief inscriptions more like accountancies of fondness, more like the times you find your bliss even in the littlest of elements of your life.

You didn't tell me that wonderland needed repair because someone had broken in, taken away its passion and madness when I would've spent every second of my life in that glitch of infinity holding in every little crack with every inch of my two hands if I could.

You didn't tell me your heart was so profound and so deep because you wanted me to notice it, you wanted me to fall into that well all on my own.

Every time that wonderland beats another breath of dust, it turns all glitters into gold,

And believe me, somewhere in the world, someone's rust is turning into those glitters of gold each time it does,

Because you didn't want Alice lost in your wonderland,

But I never minded becoming one.

12

Don't Call Me Pretty, Call Me Smart.

Tell me how the thesis of my brain intrigues your heart, mind and soul,

Let me know how caterpillar conversations of mine turn into kaleidoscopic butterflies in your stomach,

let me know if their colours are impressive enough.

How the questions of my youthful and gullible mentality create ripples of euphoria in yours,

And how those ripples show themselves in each of our smiles,

Forming threads sown right into each of our hearts.

I want you to like my mind with your heart,

To caress it with your soul.

It can assemble a beautiful palace, construct a mysterious fantasy within seconds,

I want you to just pay attention.

Listen, because only then you'd realise how I'm more than simply an appealing face,

Listen, because I trusted you enough to show you my truest introspections and beliefs.

Listen, because I have held too much innocence and delusion together tied up in my sanity and listen,

Because my spirit only seems to connect to my psyche.

I will enlighten you with the strangest hypothesis and theories,

Tell you how I believe there is a person sitting in solitude at the core of the earth,

Silently weaving a blanket of soil and dirt,

The most controvertible queries,

Most sentimental beliefs.

Look at paintings like they are alive and breathing,

And make out how in the end,

Each of them teach us to keep dreaming.

Have conversations about philosophy and life in the middle of the night,

I will tell you about my fantasies of having at least 20 dogs in a private resort in the future right before bedtime.

I will talk for hours and hours about how pixelated eyes see only watercolour skies,

Because I want you to see my eyes that way.

I want you,

To be enchanted by the complex mechanisms of my intellect,

To try to apprehend me before informing me I'm persistent and periodically insane,

To hold my mind closer to your heart than my body or my face,

Because the path to my heart's castle is found exclusively through the gateways of my brain.

13

Museum of Thoughts.

I tend to think before closing my eyes shut at any time of the day,

It's sometimes that I only close them to invite a bunch of thoughts that I had kept waiting at the back of my mind the entire time I didn't,

But one day I arranged my thoughts,

Ever so gently,

like art in a museum,

There was an art piece like the starry night except the night wasn't as dark, and the stars weren't as starry,

It looked more like a battleground between the unsettling drifting thoughts around my mind that I had grown to carry,

I carried the puzzles about philosophy because I wondered how the stars looked,

What lay after the existence of us, And as I admired it, I got dragged back to the maths problem my teacher explained too problematically for me to understand. I sighed, how do I even comprehend this?

It's rather questions that resembled stars,

and my mind that corresponded to the night,

The night was just as incredible and peaceful as ever,

And so the stars too danced notoriously around without a worry in the world.

The floor of the museum was marble, and the lights were dim,

If my mind were a place,

It would be this,

Once again,

I stopped across a piece,

A piece of my heart, or I would rather say for,

It was about all the things I'd ever loved so dearly,

I could hear the tunes of my violin coming from within it,

And see pages flying around the piece,

Pages of my favourite novels with quoted lines, and the books I only carry in my wish list, were flying around like butterflies, even butterflies could only float in front of them,

This painting was a collage, collage of text messages that made me smile, and made my heart flutter with joy, a few of them had a "congratulations" written in front of them, while others were casual little "good nights",

And every time I looked at it I could see a different face,

Faces of the people I loved, And voices I reminisced about,

But one aspect was common in all of them, the scenery I saw them in,

It was of the essence of nature, the most stunning garden, with chrysanthemums and Lillies, and bushes of the perfect shade of the perfect purple hidden in the sentiments and warmth of the lavender flowers,

I glistened in happiness and even though I wished I could caress those flowers,

hear the voice of my violin forever, and let my heart too flutter in the air like pages that were there, even though I wished I could let myself drown in that painting,

I walked away.

Maybe that is what my heaven looked like, and I wished to come back to it someday.

The following painting I saw looked like a black hole,

And it was garnished with a black colour with such darkness, it looked as if it extended till the gates of eternity, almost attractively,

Was this the meaning of "there's a beauty in darkness" I chuckled,

Yet I knew it carried my tears, trauma, sins and regrets,

maybe even that maths problem because it seemed to keep stretching to the depths of my mind,

The air surrounding the piece was cold, cold as the first day, and the last night of winter,

I'd wished I could tear that piece down, and let it vanish and wither into the same cold threatening air,

But there's no good without the bad, and no life without experience,

I sighed, not in sadness but In peace and relief,

Because there isn't any growth without acceptance,

I tenderly touched the edge of the piece, and vulnerably straightened it,

I smiled.

As far as I could visualize,

My thoughts extended to infinity, and so did the museum,

from the time I saw a honeybee in my classroom to the time I wrote my first poem,

From the time I won my first medal, to the time I cried about academic validation,

one thing was clear to me the entire time,

Imagining could allow me to bend the laws of science,

And let me do wonders,

Even while laying on my sofa and holding my iPad.

14

Wonders Too Powerful for Our Eyes to Witness.

I heard last night, we humans emit a sort of light.

A light we cannot see because our eyes are too weak,

And yet I dared to imagine how it would be,

If we could see each other as glowing bioluminescent objects of emotions,

Maybe I already do, hypothetically of course,

But have I really never seen that light?

As vaguely as I remember it I saw it in your eyes,

I couldn't give a name to that attraction,

It was so intense and deep,

but at the same time subtle and profound,

Was that love I stared so deeply into or just that light,

Just that light or attraction or tiny bits of admiration,

I could only imagine what it was,

It was bewitching and hypnotic, a little bit addicting,

It was beautiful.

It felt so strange I couldn't give a name to that allure,

How could a writer be at a loss of words?

Yet I stood there breathless, and wordless,

Some things can neither be turned into art, nor poetry,
They can only be felt, they are abstractions themselves.
I'd like to think about this wonder called love,
It exists but it's too dominant for our hearts to contain,
Hence we can merely awe in of its beauty and dance under its light,
The habits of love are, it ignites,
I must've seen that love too when I looked at you, my moon,
When I saw you, you started subsiding into pixelated white glimmers,
Standing on a cliff, my legs on the grass, my hands crossed,
I looked at you with such passion and devotion,
No, I didn't speak a word, *I found your love in silence too,*
My eyes invited tears because I knew I could never caress you,
Maybe you had swarmed those tears in my eyes through your mind, I could only imagine,
if it were true that you had done so, I would've allowed myself to cry rivers and rivers,
Just so I could feel a bit of intimacy,
That moment I felt, the only reason I stood on a cliff,
It was to be closer to the moon.
I think your eyes, they reminded me of the moon,
Your eyes? They bought out the same engulfing contentment inside me, as did the moon.

15

At My Fingertips.

The tip of my fingers, the lines of my palms,

They held a bit of strangeness today, soft ripples of calm.

They didn't tingle or prickle,

Throb my mind into a restless state, a paradoxical misconception.

Rather, I felt unusually serene,

And I could've spent hours wondering why but I was already tumbling, falling into the hypnosis of this sensation.

Like how snow falls

over a leaf in the cold and shrewd winter,

A sense of hope and wish fluctuates in the admirer as they watch,

Watch how gently it reaches the leaf with no thought of engulfing it in the piercingly cold haven,

Instead caressing it, making the leaf its newly found dwelling.

At my fingertips, I felt that serene silence, the comforting cold of the snow,

And simultaneously even the welcoming of the leaf.

A home.

We do not even realise how much our mere existence makes us shine so stupendously,

that aura that we carry within ourselves,

It's the song of the soul unique to each person.

My veins were more intricate today,

As if they danced in the bliss of liberation,

Felt an amount of levitation and then sit still in the clouds,

A bit towards the black but more towards the white,

Consuming me, I thought I witnessed a new light,

And pieces of the puzzle oddly fit together,

Pages of books became more whispers than fiction,

Your smile was more than just an emotion,

I noticed how your eyes scrunched,

When your lips formed a smile,

A rainbow on your face,

of colours and expression,

And you made my eyes sway so effortlessly.

Nothing made me feel ever so alive, alive I felt at the tip of my fingers, parts of me I cherished in the lines of my palms.

16

If I Could Describe Comfort.

If I could describe comfort, it would be the dried-out highlighters that deserve their own memorial that they never got, you might ask me the cause of death, it wasn't my intent but something just clicked in my brain, the invasions in history were no longer secrets left in vain, and silence was of the strongest domain.

Connections.

Affinities.

comfort would be solving equations so fast your hand starts to ache because it cannot pace up with the beautiful neuronal connections forming in your brain, it aches but it feels more like a reward than pain.

If I could describe comfort, it would be the dim yellow lights striking the sticky notes covering half my wall but If it were up to me, I'd cover my entire room with them. It would be the sound of ink so rigorously stroking the atoms of my page, the diffusion combining them into one, it would be murmuring chemistry reactions on page 16 in my sleep like it were a magic omen unheard. It would be the sound of nonchalant melodies bursting through my iPad, and the drowsiness of my eyes, but the voice in my head telling me to not give up, telling me there is more to subjects of physics and maths than random symbols and simple relations, telling me there are equations from the heavens above that are meant to be solved, and known, and understood.

Letting me know there's a universe inside of everything in the universe and that I wasn't meant to simply exist In mine.

17

Pixels in My Eyes.

And why do we see?

I could've answered that question with a scientific definition,

But my philosophical spectrum wouldn't stay still,

It would search through clouds,

And run through mountains,

Hypnotised by those philosophical lenses,

Observed everything probable,

To acknowledge that question.

But she couldn't find a reason so reasonable it turned this petty riddle into a mere query.

So she closed her eyes,

In awe and despair,

Desperation maybe.

Noticed pixels in disguise,

No longer was it a beetle,

Nor a cup of tea,

It was just pixels,

Black and white and red and green.

And she wondered why she saw pixels right before her vision sealed shut,

Maybe those pixels symbolised symmetry?

Because she couldn't differentiate what turned into those squares,

It was just a perfect harmony of colours,

Was it a sign that spoke of relativity between common things?

In the end, we are birthed through the same atoms.

That In the end we all just live to fulfil our appetite and thirst and bluntly enjoy our mere existence,

and maybe, if I were a beetle,

I'd live a life more beautiful,

More sane, more peaceful,

With clutches of complexity,

I felt,

we, humans, have forgotten the fundamental principles of simplicity,

And maybe it was that desire of doing more than eating and living,

That Today I'm able to type these words with utter adoration,

Because *the greatest go against and beyond the common minds of the common population,*

If the pixels symbolised our worth,

We'd all resemble diamonds,

Some big, others a tad too small,

But we'd all be together.

Shattered I felt when I realised those pixels only appeared when my eyes invited tears,

In my sadness, however,

I found another journey of philosophy.

18

The Simple Silent Epiphany.

We live in a world knotted and tied between the romantic and the pragmatic, the art and the science, there's a tug of silent and tranquil war, a feeling and delusion of harmony that even upholds the world fixed in a manner that cannot be intervened with. A poet's world is considered unconventional and strange by the pragmatic, and every philosopher, writer, artist, lover thinks that the world of these neutrality inflicted dreamers is mediocre at best. It is a mere realisation to apprehend we live in two contrasting different worlds, we live in the world of attempting to be aesthetic to seem alleviating when the real enlightenment lies in having the silent epiphany of self-realisation, in the final attainment of being content in your own company. We yield ourselves to the hollow happiness of validation from someone else. That doesn't matter in the world of day dreamers, Some may argue that romantics depend on someone or something else to feel happiness, yet real romanticism lies only in giving, only in admiring something so minuscule, someone so normal, something so ordinary, someone so normal having something so ordinary which is minuscule without wanting anything else in return. And, poets like me are so delusional, I believed that the artery that connected my heart to my index finger had ink running through instead of blood which would form such encapsulated words that would later turn into my way of giving to the world, the universe, to someone I don't even know, but that is exactly what selflessly giving is. I am a believer of science more than hypotheses, but I admire both equally. Facts intrigue me but fiction fascinates me, it makes me feel elated that how far we have come in the field of science is only because we were capable of imagining so far, because we made a speculative scenario first, because everything that exists today was only mythical once. And to achieve such hyper realistic goals, we must've had such tremendous affection and a leap of faith in science, that someone built a rocket through maths equations, someone dreamt about how the stars in the sky are not just a collection of infinitesimal dots. The most beautiful part about all that even is, the more you study science, the more you realise how normalised and primary the world is made through our sights when it is so unbelievably extraordinary through our gazes.So, the world is tied between romantic and pragmatic, artists and scientists, I like to believe there is art in science, and there is some really beautiful science in art as well, and that, that is my silent epiphany.

19

Intentionally Cultivated Mess.

Who could possibly have the eyes to witness the connections that were made when my pages were open and airy,

Afloat-like clouds floating in the sky like a kaleidoscope of butterflies,

It was a cultivated mess that I had intentionally grown on my study table,

The words I wrote were so infinitesimal that if examined, looked like ants ran over my books,

But no one ever saw how intricately I crafted each and every one of my letters,

From the word hypnotic to bewitching, they were all written in a way that was fitting.

And I had always been scolded about my texts lying open always on my desk,

But no one really understood how captivating I found it,

To see them that way is so inviting and alluring.

Knowledge lay at my fingertips,

And I for one, always surrendered to its immortality

To have the essence of words being at my sight with different fonts travelling through my eyes,

It always felt like a rite of passage,

most of the time a little more comprehensive than the rest of the world.

20

Life is But a Dream.

Imagine one day you woke up from your sleep, only to find yourself in a completely white, silent, serene and quiet room. There is no source of light from where the bright light is coming, it is just white everywhere. The room is neither cold nor warm, it is eerily the right temperature. You walk and walk for miles, trying to make sense of what's happening but you can't.

What if life truly were just a dream?

What if reality is really only a simulation? who knows, one day just an eye twitch can pull that switch holding you back from making all of this a memory. A right memory.

Don't some moments make you gasp in attraction, make your mind abandon all of its sanity and just stare at them forever? Till infinity, and you know it's not possible but the lenses in your eyes can't regain their focus as if some sort of imaginary spell has manipulated them, an attraction, a tiny pebble in the pond of depth, there is so much more to explore in these moments, to count the number of freckles her face, to see how sunlight tiptoes through the broad leaves of the trees in summer afternoons or to simply cherish the way someone smiles. Maybe these moments are the ones that feel so ethereal, you almost feel lustrous, about to fall, and get lost inside the dream till the never-ending battery of the clock in the most antique shop stops moving the hour and minute hand.

Part II

Affection.

21

It is the Way.

I think it's how sunlight renounces all its power, all its elements when it passes through that dash of rain. It is the manner my dog plays with an ant-like it's the most vibrant being she has ever seen, and that ant? it trusts her tiny little paws so much it allows itself the ecstasy and amusement of being slightly and gently caressed by something that could possibly kill it, while the eyes of my dog flicker with the bounty of enthusiasm, the ant too puzzles her paws upon where to walk next. Or perhaps it's how the clouds pave the way for the sun to shine after the rain, maybe they try to find comfort in the light scattered onto them after going through such a turbulent breakdown. The way the intricate trees I observe around my house suddenly lose all their perplexing thoughts and dance in the storm like it's all they perpetually yearned for. It's how my mom ends up fiddling and teasing my dog like she's a kid again, she almost finds the seldom escapades of her bewildered childhood hidden inside the forests of her fur, it is love. It Is admiration that I witness when I see my friend holding a book ever so gently, just as tenderly as she holds her cup of coffee, *heaven forbid one inch of that book and that cup be left unaccounted of fondness*, she finds snippets of freedom and escapes from existence in those two elements of her day and she adores it as much as she can, I find affection in my dad's smile when he brings 2 kilos of oranges just because the last time he bought some, I uttered the words *"I like them"*, the way my Nani's eyes sparkle and her cheeks blush the prettiest shade of pink at the thought of her late husband, *"till death do us part" sounds like a foreign phrase to me suddenly, star crossed lovers don't separate when they become stars themselves, do they?* The way my dog snuggles and cuddles up to me late at night, she saunters through my blanket as quietly as she can, and licks my face a little bit, greeting me as she lies sleeping up in my arms, and suddenly all the nightmares turn into ruptures of teary daydreams in my mind. I always liked my study table messy with scraps of whispery pages spread across it but I never understood why, maybe I too find comfort in catching a glimpse of pages in my books glisten towards me, knowing I will always respect them because knowledge somehow sounds to me like a synonym of heaven.

Love does not lie in words, it lies in tiny acts of appreciation, or belonging, and love, love is so profound, you don't even realise doing these acts.

22

The Flats of Your Feet.

To me, The flats of your feet flutter like a butterfly's wings as you progress down the stairs,

Yet no one realises how much you resemble one.

No one notices the smile on your face,

The childishness, the sound of laughter emerging as the radiance from your eyes

While speaking of the most bizarre topics you still sound as if reciting a mystically intriguing fairytale,

You pretend as if there is not a single thought in your head,

Yet who knows the complex mechanism of the ripples in your brain that effortlessly attract so many

Who knows your beauty as you are,

And now the heart of mine questions if there's anything it must do,

If there is any purpose it must have,

Other than finding a way between those flaps of your wings,

So desperate,

It would be content even beneath your feet.

23

Red Pretty Crystals of Love.

They say that rust destroys iron,

but I believe it's just an indication of old age,

Red pretty crystals of adoration, admiration composing on its body like love given from time itself,

So it was nice to see my necklace I was gifted 5 years ago have rust on it,

It turned from the colour of gold to rose gold, it was oxidised, and it wasn't rust that had formed, neither iron that I wore, but the colours had changed,

somewhat close to an indication maybe I had left my past self, but that ring was made for me because even if it turned to stone I would let my fingers take the weight but I would always wear it,

That rust,

It communicated like the last day I could feel my dog's heartbeat, just before she passed,

her heart maybe had rusted too much,

And I'll never be able to forget how it sounded,

prettier than pebbles when a water stream hits them, and lighter than the sound a feather makes when it reaches the ground, it sounded more intricate than the tunes of a professional violinist as if she said to me, just before she reached another dynasty,

"I love you."

And now I realise, all the appealing crystals of rust that formed in her heart in abundance,

Were not a gift from time,

But a cloak on her heart that took her to eternity.

24

I Fell for You.

Holding the last bit of their tender smile,

A name in their minds,

Depth and philosophy lose all their paths,

And you're free from reality,

What must've been the vision that you last witnessed before shutting your eyes,

That you sleep so comfortably,

At times I wonder if death is the entire comfort,

The fraction of which you witness in your sleep,

Yet what I find more appealing, is the way your eyelashes curl up,

The way your lips fall into a sweet cherished smile,

A smile that could make a million fall head over heels for you,

It is naturally beautiful.

He always smiled with his lips and she always smiled with her teeth,

Who knew a guitar would find its symphony in the mystery of a violin?

And they were perfect for each other.

It is the manner in which your eyelashes resembled the leaves to me,

Curling up and falling still, just as a leaf allows itself to blow through the wind,

You, you were spectacularly peculiar.

25

Resembled My Heart in the End

Delicacy never felt so vivid and blurry,

Yet so mystic and hypnotic.

I don't think I will even be able to explain

How the patterns in the clouds,

Reach the window steep of my room each morning,

Throw a dusty yellow light on my bedsheet

And it scatters into golden love,

Love, love, love,

Golden and shiny like crystal raindrops transformed into the prettiest necklace you'd find at a jewellery store,

The sweet kind of love,

But the inevitable part about love is that it's also the only thing with the power to kill you,

Just as the heart allows itself to be caressed,

Expectations might as well destroy it in the end.

But isn't that what we all feel?

Maybe the hands that caressed my face so sweet and warm and gentle,

Those same hands had long fingernails rough skin and pores,

Maybe I forgot to witness what I put myself under,

And when it stung I realised I was in too deep.

But I could see the light still caressing every inch of my black bed sheet,

So pure and hypnotising.

Maybe that was love too,

And,

I chose to fall into fatal mesmerism once again.

26

Love, Sapphire Gold, Love.

Love, was it sapphire gold? The one you see on a summer night, in Karaoke bars, Whispers in the library.

The sweet and perfect and playful love.

"They're romantically soulmates, platonically lovers."

Not the one you see in movies, the kind you read about in books, when the words hold you close to your heart, the yearning to find your other part,

It reaches your body like it was destined to.

You know you slept hugging that book that night in longing.

The kind of love that never rusts,

Maybe one like the squirrel who built a family on the tree planted by the old man when his wife passed away. I bet not a day passes by and he doesn't whisper

"I love you"

to that tree.

That affection still cradles the squirrel's family, and it shall for generations to come.

It is the kind of love, the warmth you feel when your own hands are cold but maybe someone else's isn't and they offer to share with you that warmth, not a matter of much thought but they offered you to touch the warmth their body took so much time to accumulate, to radiate, however, it doesn't matter to them because selflessness is only an aspect of admiration.

It's the sweet love you find in between pages of your journal one fine morning, the simple love you find in the taste of coffee or maybe just sitting in the sunlight holding someone, yourself close to you.

It's the whisper you have at the back of your mind at times,

I love you so,

So much more than the length from the earth to the moon, *I could even walk that distance to be with you.*

So much more than the days that feel like rivers have run dry, and clouds may just cry, however, *I will be faster in reaching you than the first drop of rain that reaches them,*

So much more than the prettiest clouds surrounding the sunlight, *I would be the sunflower fighting those clouds to be with your sun,*

I will long to be with you forever and ever and always. Even if it means being a mellow sunflower.

So much so that when star-crossed lovers like us become stars ourselves, *I would fight the battles and be the star that takes the fall with you as a comet,* completing every wish of every person after they see us in the sky.

So much more, more than just those three pretty words.

The sapphire gold love, it's the one that turns hearts and eyes into sapphire gold souvenirs of affection, remarkably so, it's the rarest of them all.

27

Heartbeats.

I felt her heartbeat, my dog's heartbeat And I felt gentle, I felt a need to make her feel safe, Such a wonderfully mystic part of her keeps her alive, Such a fragile part of her, and I almost imagined a crystal heart because that's what felt like love, A crystal heart with cracks of minor inconveniences, souvenirs of all that she had been through, pixelated blue blurry eyes, blurred as a tornado, but the blue ignited peace, that was the heart she had.

And the sunlight kissed her eyes, and I kissed her forehead,

I would hold her in my arms not out of love, but in an attempt of making her realise how my heart was now beating for her.

Maybe this is what love is supposed to feel like,

To be felt deeply and vulnerably and emerge as one.

28

The Branches.

The branches,

Such vivid illusionists, they seem to be,

To form a dimension within the leaves,

And as I walk past that delusion,

I can't help but notice the intricacy,

The reality that birthed that imagination,

Leaves, thousands I couldn't grasp,

They shaped a part of me,

Maybe they were the rib cages of the trees,

And I was standing still at the heart,

Crushing and clasping but not suffocating,

The feisty kind of love, the playful one,

And the ones that are more separated,

They look more like the soft kind of love,

The love that lies only in summer,

Lovers that love with a love that is more than love.

Yet even the depth and dominance of winter couldn't separate them,

And when there was rain,

The dark only surrendered to their love,

Profoundly and so, magnificently,

It looked like an elixir of magic in the sky,

Rather than the demonic beast it was meant to be,

Sometimes people can only awe and envy your beauty,

Looked just as messy as the 2nd grader's paint splattered on his page,

He did not care how it looked,

And that was the definition of the universe,

The sky bounds the clouds and the sun,

Most imperfections have minute patterns of perfection,

And I cannot help but notice them,

Keep them as souvenirs at the back of your mind,

Witnessing miracles of the divine.

29

Mornings.

I never quite understood why people didn't like mornings so much.

The way sunlight wanders inside your bedroom through your window panel, your window so pristine it looks crystalline, the sunlight tries to hypnotise your soul into absolute oblivion yet each time it does, the warmth grasps you and more often than always, you definitely find solace. *Peace. Serenity.* If hope was ever a sensation, a sentiment you felt through a real-life instance, you knew it would be your morning.

After nights that feel endless and dreams that you don't want to end, you find a snapshot, a portrait at the back of your mind of a chrysanthemum blooming in the sunlight in a field of lavenders, and that's what mornings make you feel like. Unapologetically that chrysanthemum which always grows taller but its petals never grow wider so it camouflages perfectly in the field of lavenders,

Constantly feeling like an imposter but in the mornings, you acknowledge the fact that maybe you're just extraordinary.

The sway in your hips, the subtle smile on your lips, the flutter in your feet, you dance with your headphones on as you saunter across the room making note of every slight crease on your sunlight-inflicted bedsheet,

Secretly, you like it.

You like feeling in control, you like to correct and caress and ever so gently touch the sheets and tug them in the corner that has practically never ever dusted, you like to fluff up your pillows and like to make sure they nearly look like a butterfly's wings, so spirited.

And it's the best part of your day suddenly when you reach the kitchen and make your first cup of coffee, hold it like it's a hug to yourself, that one mug of yours just makes you pleased instantly.

You sit in the sunlight for a while now, you've hated when things you've always loved end but somehow, you don't mind if your morning does.

You're so in love with it, you know it'll come back tomorrow too.

But you also can't help but hope one day it's not just the mornings that make you feel so remarkable.

30

Why Cover Your Heart?

Why do you strip off metal wires and sheets of aluminium and hold your heart inside that very confined space so much so it no longer breathes the mesmerising song it always has, why do you jot it down bit by bit, your thoughts too, speculate everyone like they're old statutes, but darling you forget sometimes, you weren't supposed to be a historian.

I know it is not easy but at times its more about giving than receiving, because expectations can be deceiving.

I know it hurts when the people you love are the ones that were leaving but you need to raise your chin up and give your heart more love,

Do not suffocate it inside a plastic wrap just because it gave too much.

Your heart is not just a heart, it's a fountain of feelings and thoughts,

And if you choose to shut that wonderland out of the world,

Then really, what is the difference between you and a criminal not caught?

You are so incredible and gorgeous, and so very pure and kind,

So be that way with the people that surround you,

With the gifts that are around you.

Not because you want something in return,

But because your soul asks you to be,

Because you're concerned if that one person is disappointed in their results,

If their feelings are hurt.

If your loved ones are faking their smile,

If they've had a good laugh in a while.

You're worried about everyone else sleeping with a full stomach,

Including your furry friends,

Because their voices are often not heard,

their words are not easy to apprehend.

It is okay if you show that kindness, ask those tiny questions of concern,

It's a hug to yourself, poetry to some.

A sentiment of care, but not dependency,

So remove the plastic wrap and let your heart flourish as the garden that was always there,

Because the ones who are ready to face the storm with a smile on their face,

Are the ones who can find love and happiness,

Laughter and contentment,

anyhow and anywhere.

31

All That Leads to Love.

Do we eventually just become who or what we love too?

Does a poet become his poetry?

words of fiction, existing in the realm of reality,

Do all the poems come to life in their minds eventually,

Engulfing their mind and soul as a whole if it wasn't already ready to be stretched and broken apart and let to fly and reach things far beyond the mellow skies,

Let go of your imagination and you'll realise this world too is a simulation.

Does an artist eventually become his very own art too?

No, not confined to the corners of the canvas,

Do they in the end just become their own muse,

Their paints and their strokes?

So when each time they walk down the very same road where they saw their first inspiration,

The birds in the far-stretched sky, till infinity,

One day just realise maybe their minds are the universe closer to them than the one they are living in,

And that, that is when they realise they are magic.

32

There's a Universe Inside of Everything in the Universe.

Infinitesimal number of universes inside this universe, yet the cosmos of my mind seems to only be attracted towards yours.

I do ponder sometimes if universes were made up of momentary and endearing stories ultimately reaching to the brim of heaven in the human intellect, an indefinite collection of uttered sentences that made their way from another's lips to the haven of the heart of someone else.

I do wonder if they choose to stay or are pulled In like a breath of fresh air.

It is also a paradox how close the human mind is to the absoluteness of the universe we live in so naturally and giftedly it's almost precarious, how there are millions if not billions of neurons in our brains creating infinitely many connections this present second, how the mind doesn't seem to stop bringing out thoughts intertwining them into something deeper and profound every given second, to the point that nothing ever seems stagnant or sane anymore.

What even comes close to being compared to the ever-expanding cosmos for me, is poetry and love.

Not poems, or stories, but poetry.

And perhaps I am only for one only an admirer of words, of sentences but if that were the case, I would only be a reader, a writer, a poet.

But I have experienced poetry.

I have felt how it's like to feel your thoughts become beautiful little clouds raining down a galore of emotions on you.

Have felt my fingers turn into broad leaves, my arms resembling the stems,

Have imagined so intensely that the glass of water looks as if an alive and breathing elixir.

I have imagined your love to be a person, a perfectly beautiful person with skin so clear, he's an angel.

But I can assure you the depths of my mind never crossed imagining your hatred as a devil.

I, however, have imagined the devious smile and notorious thoughts of the honeybee that entered my class on a bright sunny morning.

And have felt your soul reach mine, greeting it with a hug without even seeing you.

I have felt an Infinite amount of such experiences and I do not know if they found a place in my brain, but they gave me an image, a picture I could hold back forever in my mind and pour out words till even infinity can't hold them anymore.

I believe it's admiration, it's love and love so whole it consumes my entire being.

It is poetry,

My definition of love, *if I ever had the means to define it.*

33

I Wish My Eyes Could Take Pictures.

I wish my eyes could take pictures, and create the utopian vision I keep hidden in the pixels of the imaginary camera.

And now the smallest of elements would have so much prominence, not prominence as in they'd be bugged more focused and concrete, prominent as in, their imagines would be brighter,

They would glow and maybe neon lights would bend and twist and curve into perfect little ribbons surrounding their entire body.

There would be ribbons made of neon, and art everywhere, it won't be a utopian vision, it would be my fantasy altogether.

Suddenly, I would be able to click a snapshot of art each time I looked around,

Each time I would see those trees with their perplexing branches that looked to me to stretch till the matrix of infinity, maybe if my eyes would be able to click a snapshot of that picture, I would be able to that sight till eternity.

Each time I'd see the mess of books on my study table, in my library, maybe I'd be able to draw out how they mean something more than just turned pages with rusted edges,

How they're passageways to parallel universes, how each of them symbolises a tiny little gate, a miniature escape to another world.

Maybe I would be able to click a shot of that.

If my eyes could take pictures, *I'd perhaps spend more time with you than I should trying to capture every breathtaking vision of yours I keep to myself.*

34
Unexpectedly Affectionate.

I see traces of moss and fern on every red rustic brick path I walk upon,

Green and yellow, with the softest touch it caresses the bricks and the stones almost trying to grasp them into its attention,

Inclination never felt so submerging.

Submissiveness of course is only a strand of love.

Only a part of its utopia.

But the inclination to the extent you forget you have a colour of your own,

Causes nothing but disaffiliation,

To see a person through the filter of your eyes,

Governed by your eyelashes,

It is not the happy bliss of dancing under the moonlit dimension of admiration,

Rather its almost as careless as dancing in the paradise of a fool,

a master manipulation even in some rare instances.

"Unconditional love"

that same love can be found in these bewildered traces,

the disorientation in itself,

The way the bricks allow themselves to be hypnotised by the moss and the fern,

And yet somehow manage to look so exceptionally old, so morally right.

There is no realistic symmetry,

But in an abstract sense?

Maybe love is not meant to be found in bewilderment,

Because it is so inexplicable itself.

35

Curiosity Amplifies When the Mind's Still Young.

So I guess I was fairly critical of how unexpectedly love can grow,

Curiosity amplifies when your mind is still young,

And then I looked at moss and fern,

growing in the bricks of the old man's house after his wife passed away, a sense of belonging,

Or in the river where the fishes sang a virtuous song,

it formed tiny little spots of pleasant memories and gateways to what was under the water,

It is found underneath trees where love blossoms and blooms,

Where two squirrels decided to build a family,

And where the maternal nest of a bird stays,

It is even found at hospitals with people bidding their farewells,

When people go to the other dimension,

Found in airports where kisses of romantic soulmates, and platonic lovers ignite the room,

The beauty of it all is, it is unexpected

It is pure attraction, purely intricate and stitched into destiny by the divine.

36

When I Tell You That I Love You.

I mean to say that you could mean to me just as much as the happiness I find noticing an ant that lost its way somehow reaching back its line.

I mean to say that your presence makes me as happy as when I don't have to slash off a perfectly written word because it finally doesn't have the wrong spelling,

Sometimes I swear the curvature of the letter "c" my fingers drew matches the curve of your eyelashes in the morning dew.

I mean to say that I am so smitten by you, almost as much as I am by the complex equations of mathematics that perplex my brain, they are quite challenging but that's probably why I love them so much.

I mean to say that I think I love you as much as I love it when my favourite song comes to play when I shuffle my playlist, I love you as much as I love the smell of caramelised onions in ghee, maybe I do, I love you as much as I see art, even more, when I see the artists that made the art in their art, they leave a piece of themselves in it. I love you as much as I like to see opera houses and hope to visit one someday. I'll take you with me, with me to every library in the world. I love you as much as that. I love you as much as I love to wrap my hands around warm mugs in the winter season, like I'm hugging them because they make my fingers feel so comfortable.

When I tell you that I love you, I will hope to meet you like I hope someone would put a warm blanket over my cold feet when I end up falling asleep on the sofa in winter.

That I will admire you as I admire the Gulmohar tree that shades my house,

I'll confess my love so much and so many times and so spontaneously, like how I get so excited when I see any dog outside my home and instantly tell it that it means the entire world to me because its eyes look so heavenly.

If you give me your heart,

I will take care of it as I care for my dog when she falls asleep in my blanket in the morning, and I pick her up ever so gently because I don't have the audacity to take away the sweet smile on her face while she sleeps.

No, I won't be able to promise you the world, *but I will be able to give you my world.*

I'll give you my hypothetical solar system of the people that I love and admire, and maybe one day you'll find your position there as the sun.

I don't write about love much,

But when I tell you that I love you,

I think it means that maybe I'll end up writing about you too.

37

The Beauty of Fragility.

"How beautiful it feels to be so fragile"

A flower could be easily plucked away from the Gulmohar tree that shades my house,

Yes, its leaves are fragile, and so are its branches,

But if I were to pick up on every single flower and branch I could gather from the tree,

I would be challenging myself,

Because when I observed that tree for the first time,

I noticed how intricately it was made,

And even though I wished to count the number of branches there were,

The leaves it carried,

The flowers it caressed,

It was so complex I couldn't,

Because after a while it looked as if the branches tangled up with each other till infinity,

It look so delicate I questioned at a point how it carried even one of its leaves,

The branch was facing downwards but the flower facing up,

It carried the flower like it was made of feathers,

With petals so soft and light, it made it look like the flowers of that tree were In love with the force of gravity,

And gravity allowed them to glisten in the sky,

To enjoy the freedom and the depths of being young and naive and free.

I fell in love with every single branch,

Or did I rather wish to,

A fragile heart like mine desperate to find a lover in a tree,

Sounds ridiculously relatable to me.

But I cannot contain the compassion I carry in my heart,

Neither could I contain the feeling of having my heart bloom similar flowers later that day.

Like a tiny pinch of what heaven feels like,

God left us, love,

Love in our hearts.

They say geniuses often go crazy,

Is it because they fall in love far beyond the means of our comprehension?

I like to believe that.

Because sometimes when contemplating love,

nothing seems sane,

or normal,

or simple,

When we look for answers about things from the beyond.

Maybe, we aren't meant to look at all.

38

When I Die, I Wish to Die Naturally.

Death

I watched the Titanic 5 times, no not because of Jack and Rose, I believed they would reconcile in heaven, and god wouldn't be so ruthless.

Instead, I observed how the ship sank into the deep cold water, it was tragic. Like the river engulfed people wholly, they were destroyed but honestly, that didn't scare me, yet even the slightest utter about somebody being murdered mercilessly, I had shivers down my spine. Of course, I had to speculate this.

So,

When I die,

I wish to die "*naturally*",

Be buried inside the earth,

The way I was birthed,

And even if the tides would play the villain in my story,

I would find a company, nurture,

The tides would carry me to a place of absolute peace, harmony,

And I would not die in vengeance,

Because I don't have the heart to hate something so marvellous,

So enigmatic, even though it led to my demise,

I would feel my mother's warmth and tenderness in the waves,

It wouldn't hurt me, instead'd feel privileged that I died holding the contentment of the ripples of water in the lines of palms, I would feel loved.

If I were given only a day to live,

I would spend my time strolling through the gardens,

Stroking invisible air that walked with me like a playmate through my life,

I would try to grasp the scent of a rose, a chrysanthemum, a lotus, every flower I could,

And memorise it so that in heaven I would breathe the love of nature every day,

And when the clock would strike 11:30,

I would lay still on the ground of my gardens,

Wearing my favourite rosy pink dress,

Hands-free and legs apart,

I would stare at the sky,

The glamour in each of the stars,

Imagine my eyes were a telescope that could see the most radiant of nebulae,

darkest of black holes,

And smile.

Let creepers and flowers travel all over my body,

Blossom me with comfort,

And pull me inside the earth,

I would only look at my side to see the drop of water on the leaf of grass closest to me,

It might rain,

"Maybe nature cried killing me, a person with such admiration about it"

Even the suffocation would feel like tears of satisfaction to me.

39

Little Moments of Joy.

I always thought I couldn't find happiness in someone else's, But the way I smiled when my dog played with its food as she admired it more than anything I could ever admire, god was I happy. I still wonder why and how that even made me smile so hard, so much when she turned topsy and turvy playing with it here and there. What was going on at the back of her mind, was it a debate going like "Should I eat this or should I not?" Knowing well enough that she would get the exact same food the next day yet she appreciated it so much it felt that it was the last time she'd get to taste such food, such food with equivalent taste to how the clouds tasted, I imagined she might be thinking "I think this is how those cotton candy clouds would taste, and those flowers that were at such height I couldn't reach to eat them" what was it going so profoundly in her mind that she had such simple happiness about something I'm guilty of considering so mere.

I had grown to believe I couldn't find happiness in someone else's,

But what about that time in the grocery store when I saw three young boys talking about how much money they had to choose the type of juice they wanted to have, and how they were so proud and happy and eager at the same time the billing counter, my little heart couldn't handle the number of hopes they had for that one bottle of juice and the purest smiles I had ever seen they made while they took it with them outside, I smiled so much, and it felt that their purity rubbed off on my face, yes I had my own worries, but looking at them, I realised how different things mean differently to different people. It might be very easy for me to get that bottle of juice but I was pretty sure they had to use their pocket money for it and the amount of hope they put into how it would taste. Oh if it were up to me, I would've bought them the whole rack just to see them smile and jump and let their little hearts flutter with such heaps of excitement! and it wasn't only their smiles that made me smile, it was how their eyes reflected the hopes in their hearts and the love in their hands as they so tenderly held that bottle.

It's the thing about hopes and expectations, people say that to be happy, you must not have expectations from things or people and just do your part, I counter that thought. No, not when you're a kid so eager and wild and you don't care the least about global warming or a career or the world. Your world stays still and concentrated on your favourite snack you cherish the most or in the midst of your first bicycle or the first time you see a staircase and walk it up in an instant just to slowly walk down in harmony with gravity, heck you don't even know the principle of gravity it's just the comfort of the steps on your shoes, that makes your heart race a 100 times faster than it was in such utter happiness you really couldn't care much about anything. It's just the heaps of excitement I think, that made me happy. It's the curiosity of discovering the world for the first time that made me smile, I found happiness in your happiness and you didn't even realise, I'm grateful that the bottle of juice made you so happy that I cherished it myself without tasting it. desire is so versatile. I think I was wrong when I called myself selfish for not being happy at someone else's happiness, I think I insulted myself as a philosopher, and a writer when I said that. Because when I grow up to have a busy life and a busy career, I hope I can buy a rack of goodies for boys that reflect the three boys I saw when I was fourteen, I hope that I can thank the universe for the happiness they gave me even if unknowingly. And I hope that I still have the silent company of my dog, except for when I give her food, I hope I too have just even half the excitement she has for such mere things, I hope not only do I have that, I have her right beside me, her playing with the food and adoring it and I wish at that very moment I look at my plate of whatever food I'm having, and smile.

My personal ambitions and Desires can reach heights, but I hope that my sense of what I call happiness stays as simple and down-to-earth as possible, I would love that when I'm older.

40

Inspirational Lamps.

There was a dim yellow light that was exhibited from the lamp kept in my parent's bedroom, a light so genuine and phenomenal that whenever people smiled under it, it looked as if they laughed, so mesmerising that my dad's skin looked glittery in colour whilst my mom's rosy pink.

I loved reading my favourite books underneath its conventionally beautiful light,

And start to believe that the words were falling off of the pages in my book, that I was in a wonderland completely hooked, *I would imagine I was the black and white font in the book,* and the light would engulf my mind and soul while easing me into thoughtlessness as a whole.

But one day, it suddenly stopped.

It stopped radiating that peaceful blissful light it always did and people in my house wondered and twisted their heads, it wasn't the faulty wiring or the electricity.

It was a default within the lamp that made it stop.

That same night, hours after it stopped working, there was a sudden flicker at 3 am and I quickly got up scared, a tiny, just a tiny flick and then it was gone again.

The next morning, it flicked again for 2 seconds and then it was gone again.

The same continued for many days,

Just a tiny flicker of light.

What kept me intrigued the entire time was, no matter the faults, no matter the internal disbalance it must be going through, I didn't stop trying to keep up the light,

And even though it's just a lamp, there are many of us with that same light. But with the defaults too.

Yet we keep trying and trying all over again,

And if you ask me, *that's commendable in itself.*

41

What Are the Noble Pursuits of Life?

In the dead poets society, it was mentioned that the noble pursuits of life include law, engineering, medicine, etc. but poetry, romance, love are what we live for.

So, We don't live for hope, we simply live for faith.

But is faith that simple?

Is faith not staying up nights working on numericals that won't ever help you in the pragmatic way of things but you know this is meant to be knowledge of the beyond, that the clues in those very fine few numbers hold the secrets of the universe known to mankind, and the magnificence strikes you with the scent of esteem, scribbling on the paper till your fingers run out of breath, till your hands start tearing up, but the Enlightenment of the mind is so sacred, these things go unnoticed or are rather more appreciated.

is faith not working to the bones to find a purposeful way of life, to find a reason to live?

Is that all hope?

On the contrary, I believe it's hope, hope that makes us love, that makes us yearn for attention and belonging, that makes us want the knowledge of the fact that maybe someone could ever get so intertwined with me that we walk the path of life together, that I do not find a place in heaven or hell alone, that there is someone, just someone there.

Having the ability, the honour to call someone,

My beloved.

You are my beloved, my soul, my breath,, the way my heart pounds and my voice shakes in the loneliest of nights, you are the reason I survive those nights, the reason I choose to live more than exist.

How beautifully those words would ignite passion in someone's heart, a hope, that they would find their way to flow through even the finest of capillaries spread in the human body.

Is it not hope?, when a beautiful scenery attracts you, and the words tumble out of your lips,

"I wish we'd stay forever like this."

For, many believe forever doesn't exist.

Yet, as a person who admires science and reasoning above all,

I believe forever exists,

Let me rephrase myself,

I hope forever exists.

I hope somewhere in the universe on a planet not so far away, there does exist forever, because the universe after all is infinite, I hope, that time wraps around itself somehow to make a circle instead of a linear line, I hope time becomes infinite too, I hope it is possible that forever exists.

All for the cryptic faith hidden in the pages of my favourite books or for the hope that I dwell in my lovers' eyes, all so I have the image of the scenery constructed forever in my mind?

Is it a noble pursuit of life, to love so dearly? to admire so passionately?

It's a gift, an honour, of being human, above nobility.

42
Molten Iron

You hold me so close to you at all times.

You hold me so close as if, if you let go of me and my fragile heart, it would melt away like a heavy breath. The thing is, my heart is like molten iron, it is hot and furious and aggressive and fierce and assertive, and all things one should be not capable of. But when I told you my brain and my heart are not normal, you replied to me in the sweetest voice

"Of course they aren't, darling, they are so special."

And the pink tint rested upon my cheeks as your soft gaze did on my eyes.

The thing is, you know my heart is molten iron but you are ever so ready to hold it in your palms, and bear the heaviness, instead of everyone who kept it so sacred between their bare teeth and called me too much when the blood squirted out.

And I was the one getting wounded.

You were never afraid of getting burnt, a faint smile would appear on your face everytime it accidentally hurt but,

You'd never ever let go.

Healing things you'd never break, you'd ask me if my voice had the faintest of quakes

"Are you alright?, you don't sound okay."

And no I was not okay,

And I couldn't always pretend,

So I let my heart bare over your chest, without the anguish of bone and skin,

I articulated what I truly felt,

And you embraced me tightly in your arms, and told me,

The most ethereal sensation you've ever had,

Was to feel the grief and philosophy embedded in my heart of iron finally *melt.*

43

You Asked Me the Colour of Your Eyes.

I told you how I seek perpetuity in them, I told you how the pupils present in them grasp my soul, scavenging my sanity, twisting my actuality and challenging my morality, and suck me unto them every time I look at you whole. How you don't just have brownish-black eyes, how they seem to elude into undersized black holes that carry mysticism, the brim of enchantment in them, how they made me fall for you tumbling upon the time I was present in. I said that my room feels so empty sometimes, that even if I cried my whole life in it, I'd question if the walls of my room were the only ones without ears, and you told me, that you would hide me under the bliss of your comfort, under the mantle of your warm arms, and the scent of your body that I would no longer feel heard but understood. You told me, you would accept me and fondle my grief with teary eyes and a ruptured mind when I felt that it was an uninvited guest anywhere else I went, even within the walls of own room, even in the doors of my own house.

So, you asked me the colour of your eyes,

And I would've spent an infinity amount of time,

In the infinitely many parts of the universe,

And still have struggled to answer that,

Because how could I?

When I'm so busy losing myself in the mist of your comfort.

Part III

The Truth.

44

Blind Faith.

Oh how gracefully and profoundly she stood,

Into the ray of hope,

The light seemed largely scavenging her eyes

searching for her deep and darkened soul,

Since she had fooled many about how her soul looked,

Nobody quite knew the real truth,

Yet the sunlight seemed to comprehend all the paths and all the ways leading right into her heart, many, and maybe that is why when she stood briefly for a minute,

Eyes closed but pupils still dilated,

It looked as if the golden hour sucked the soul out of her,

Shimmers of gold and dust of yellow and orange,

A tint of pink and she looked like a goddess,

One not without a face but a mixture of paints,

An abstract painting a person needed to scrutinise intensely to understand,

She looked so mesmerizingly indifferent.

A person without a face? But she looked as if gold had accumulated each speck of her skin and now it was it's turn to take it away into infinity along with the Sunrays,

How charming she stood as if it was a rite of passage,

A heavenly gate had opened just for her,

And she contemplated whether to walk on those devious steps,

she could be mistaken,

Possibly being led to hell.

But the way the rays hypnotised every atom in her body to be sucked into nothingness,

Created nothing but a dilemma of obliviousness in that woman.

And no one really saw,

But I did,

She walked up the stairs for miles and miles,

No hope of leaving.

No sound of cries.

Still unknown to the fact that no matter how much she tried,

It was never god she would meet,

A sinister smile would greet her,

Along with a basket of lies.

45

Time is An Illusion?

Our minds resemble the sand sitting still in an hourglass,

Blended in the middle, and our mouths we can't stop.

Stop looking into the darkened hole,

But we're ready to accept our fate and walk into it like a twisted fairy tale,

But oh my love don't you know?

How Alice ended up in wonderland, lost her way forever, she let go,

And she couldn't find a reason,

led in under desperate confusion,

Her darling self lost her mind in consensus,

And maybe that was the thrill of it all,

Because how are you truly free,

if you've not met questionable decisions made in superlative instances,

And I believe that all we ever wish for is to jump just like her,

Not a wince or cry for help, not a worry in the world.

Easy to lose all emotions and travel like there's no end,

No hope of leaving either, finding nothing may be the best joy of life,

And that was what darling Alice once had believed,

But, It is not easy to read between the lines when the lines keep twisting themselves.

Sometimes those same lines build vivid hypnosis,

So unique that your soul gets sucked into nothingness,

And you don't even realise.

Even though reality seems too hungry for logic,

Unconscious palaces have no doors that open themselves for you,

The only thing pulling you back from falling deep in is that helplessness isn't the most ravishing feeling of all.

46

Into the Mirror, She Fell.

A touch would mean a spark,

And the silver lining could mean something more,

possibly dangerous too,

Yet she stood before a mirror,

Questioning the one she saw.

With eyes so perfect, and features so sharp,

She wondered if her being had finally found a guardian angel.

Every time she tried to touch her,

She touched back,

Every time she spoke,

She spoke back,

As if she was mimicking her.

It felt like an unreal connection,

The ones without an explanation,

The ones that as more destined than coincidental,

And she did not realise it then, but she had peeked into a part of herself,

Finally pictured her soul, her mind and heart.

That was the paradox of her mirror.

She saw how beautiful the one who stood before her looked,

When she didn't know she was looking at herself,

She had no way to judge her or to criticise,

Pure compliments and merely attraction,

And when she stepped closer, the way her eyes lit up,

Closer, the way her hands twitched,

Closer, at the way her breath sounded,

Closer, and closer and closer.

She fell into the mirror,

Sharp edges, blended and twisted lines,

Obsession with radiant eyes,

She fell into a puddle of "how do I look?" And tell me I look pretty, if not why,

And now when she realised, the woman was her,

She nitpicked everything inch of her skin until it resembled a plain white canvas with scraped off acrylics,

Pitiably so, just like most of us,

I can only wonder if she found valleys of narcissism inside that mirror,

Or the drowning well of insecurities.

47

A Token of Regret.

Grief, I have witnessed it so closely, and each time I do, I wish I could feel as if I was greeting a friend. But it feels more like running away from home, with a stranger.

It claims to be a token of love, but its eyes chant to me the melancholy tune of deep regret. And to be fair, so many are scared to witness its eyes because they wish to hide away from reality. It forms a paradox in the mind consisting of maybe's and what if's, and leaves us all twirling like a fool in ifs and buts. Even its voice sounds like whispers through creaky staircases and vague images.

Grief hurts even though it doesn't mean to, but maybe sometimes that hollow feeling of hopelessness because you know even if you had the power of bringing that person back, you won't. It is necessary. It is composed of love, passive. Grief is a reward of love, but a token of regret because when you love someone, time stretches itself into valleys of flowers and sunset skies hoping it would stay like that forever, sort of like when you imagine how heaven looks like, hours feel like seconds and every second you don't spend with that person feel so pricklish in your heart when that person is gone away, it is a token of regret.

Yet still a reward of life because feeling grief is necessary, celebrating the immortality of the dead, it is the grief we feel.

48

Deceptive Attraction.

The misty clouds of depth,

A speck of darkness,

A special dust of glitter,

And a river falling through your eyes,

A face made of dust in the middle of the street,

I believe I found my philosophical lenses,

Even the roads I passed suddenly had trees whose branches immersed into one another,

Almost evolving into a whole,

I questioned if that's how two souls fall in love,

Do they become united that way?

a puzzle piece for one another?

Or a chessboard of battles and scars,

the way the branches created patterns in the sky,

Black and white squares started looking familiar,

The branches further looked as if they were caressing, fondling, nuzzling and teasing each other,

they looked as if they had the sapphire gold love,

The one you hear through whispers in the library, and smell after the first drop of rain; it is the one you find in midnight snacks, or as I do in the blurry blue pupils of the winter sky.

The leaves which were falling on the road were rewriting their spirits through their colours, from green to brown to the most antique golden one could witness,

It was sapphire gold,

I believe every life has a soul,

and I was sure of it when I saw those two soulmates,

they weren't just colliding, their souls were melting into one another,

It could've been fate or destiny or even mere attraction,

The flowers looked like souvenirs of affection, warmth and admiration they shared as they fell creating watercolour skies,

It was pink and violet, a brush of blue, a nudge of yellow in the clouds,

A child's painting.

In my breaths, I could sense lavender,

The trees were like mistletoes, but they had found one another.

But as I wandered towards them captivated by their love,

I realised the fresh scent of lavender started to fade slightly,

even though it ignited the feeling of abstraction within me,

It wasn't the same.

The canopy they created caused no sunlight for me to witness as I stood right in between their bond,

I stood right underneath their branches, in their heart,

And suddenly no longer could I see the blossoming madness and uproar you see between two young lovers,

More like a mysterious masquerade,

With faults of darkness and steps of secrets,

As if the leaves hid everything yet still blended perfectly well,

A peculiar catastrophe,

So maybe the pattern I saw in the sky was a chessboard, a battle fought for eternity,

I almost felt as if I existed in the middle of a war,

And Petals fell on top of me, but not flowers,

Separated yet still blooming,

Clinging to a hope that maybe just maybe love isn't the mayhem I was witnessing,

My heart did too,

The stems intertwined with each other looking as if they were choking, or fighting one another, stems I thought were souls melting into each other,

I felt melancholy,

Leaves had a dark shadow dancing on top of them,

And the scent of fresh lavender had completely faded away

Just the imagination of my bewildered mind tried to linger on the pages of what I had seen before,

Maybe love, it is supposed to look this way,

Maybe this isn't love at all.

49

We All Live in Bubbles.

When I see people,

I see scars and stories,

millions and millions of them walking miles and miles,

Or travelling miles and miles,

I think nobody realises that looking at the road is justifiably peeking into everyone's souls,

I've always read that eyes speak things words never can,

That eyes express things words cannot,

And it may be found quite strange to some,

But I can't help and end up noticing each time I'm on the road,

A Walking stranger's eyes,

A walking heartbreak, a perfectionist, a survivor, aren't we all survivors at some level?,

I could only question as I saw the old man walking past my car,

His skin was freckled with dust of gold,

But gold isn't always glitter, sometimes it pretends to be,

Just like how heartaches pretend to be tattoos carved on your skin,

Scars pretend to be birthmarks as you say them,

But The mind fails to hide, to hide its battles, and it's always visible in the eyes,

The eyes, oh they are the windows to a soul,

And every time I'm on the road, I end up peeking inside,

it is only a glimpse of the eyes I get while travelling in a car,

the wheels of my vehicle do not keep pace with the thoughts in mind,

My thoughts still work faster than the wheels,

And I unusually feel,

"I think I sensed something in her smile" but I will never get to see her again,

I get that unusual feeling when I slash off a perfectly written word in my notebook because it is not correct,

Maybe I try to find bits and pieces of myself in others,

So I do not feel that only I have been given this life,

Deep down I know my efforts are useless,

Yet my eyes still trying to travel faster than my car,

Because they want to search for eyes,

Eyes that provide my own comfort of knowing, just knowing.

Are my eyes after all just lonely? Maybe They seek comfort.

It is just the fact that we all are the main characters in our own lives,

That makes me feel so overwhelmed, not that it is supposed to,

But to imagine that we all live in separate bubbles and you're no less than a particle of dust bypassing that bubble is fascinating

50

A Little Towards the Black, a Little Towards the White.

Daylight, hundreds and thousands and millions of clusters,
Clusters of sunshine, and even moonlight,
There existed bad in the good, good in the bad,
I sauntered through my heart, I realised.
I realised contamination sometimes skims through your eyes, and your nose,
As if was falsely manipulating you,
It could turn into whatever shape it pursued,
And it could walk through your body, all your senses and morals.
I was used to it, to the contamination, before I could even realise it,
Too much sanity feels contaminated,
Yet even the speck, even the tiniest idea of insanity provides me comfort,
And I started doubting myself.
Thoughts travelled back and forth in my mind like an aeroplane ready to take off but the engine keeps demolishing,
That noise that it makes when you're on the plane,
I felt like I was breathing that noise,
suffocating at an entirely different level.

I was contaminated.

My mind could not feel, it was numb,

While my body remained sensitive the most to my surroundings,

As if every time I touched the cold ice,

It numbed my fingers, but I still kept feeling pain.

I couldn't leave it, there was no escape,

Numbness never felt so beautiful,

While pain never felt so uncomfortable.

It was like my mind had suddenly started evaporating into the air,

A phenomenon in which my brain had drowned,

It always evaporated,

I hated it,

But I couldn't stop it either,

To travel through numbness is one thing,

But Living in a constant state of Comfort,

Of evaporation,

It was not living,

It was dancing in a paradox, your foot is wheels and your body is just a tiny little cage carrying the demons in your mind.

Where do I find happiness?

Tightly packing my smile, the prettiest shade of sunshine,

But I too endure the depths of moonlight.

I too live in between the back and the white.

51

Heavily Panting Does Not Feel Like Breathing.

Sometimes holding on too tight creates lines of designated suffocation battling with the lines of your palms, consuming them that they are indeed real,

It's really just drowning in your own submissiveness,

Overthinking, and overloving turn into a spiral of overwhelming emotions and you cannot pick yourself up because you're already so drowned,

It all ends up in titters and tatters eventually, ends up in misery,

Ends up in you losing yourself, forgetting your worth,

Ends up in you burning yourself in the fire with all your wounds open,

It ends up in a spiral you cannot escape because you put the end of the spiral in your own mouth, you. You are now subjected.

The thing is,

you tied yourself to the rock and pushed your own self into the puddle which gains water on its own, and turns into an ocean before you realise,

It turns into that sprained neck you wake up with if you sleep on the wrong side,

Except, now it's present 24/7 in all parts of your mind and body,

And the only way to escape is to provide yourself with happiness,

The happiness of suffocating yourself with one hand while letting someone else sip hot water from your other palm,

That is why heavily panting, heavily loving someone, doesn't feel like breathing.

52

The Death of the Better.

I witnessed the death,

I noticed the death of a budding artist when my teacher tore his page,

The page containing his soul, and purpose,

His art, a spectrum of enchantment,

I believed he was an abstractionist,

The way he held his pen, with such precision,

No one would believe that his paintings didn't make much obvious sense, it all depended on perception,

But was I only the one who saw depth in that page,

Depth containing marvels we can't imagine, feel or speculate,

It was mesmerising,

Was my teacher blind she so ruthlessly tore that page,

Telling him books he should concentrate on,

It was the death of an artist I witnessed that day.

I witnessed the death of a woman,

a woman so spectacular the world would've kneeled before her,

Thoughts so magnificent,

And eyes containing the fire,

But she was married off to a family where she couldn't do anything,

Where she wasn't allowed to leave the house,

To speak up,

Or to even breathe,

She was a strong lady,

but age-old oppression,

This led to loss of expression,

Patriarchy yet again had its way,

And she was locked inside a cage,

A house she couldn't leave,

Even to this date,

She's not truly free.

I witnessed the death of humanity,

When he runs that car over a puppy,

He said he didn't see it,

But were its whimpers so fluent they sounded like the harmony in the air,

Was he deaf or blind?

His mistake cost a life,

A life worth of gold,

Of happiness, and love,

Now when its mother cries,

With teary eyes,

You don't know how to apologise,

Saying that it's just a dog,

Will only lead to the creation of oppression,

Of insanity because you will set an example,

That this,

It's fine.

It's not.

Society keeps drowning further inside the water,

Such things that are considered "normal",

Are truly carelessness, and misuse of power.

I hope one day I sit still and write pages and pages,

About how everything has changed,

If that woman wouldn't have been locked up,

Maybe society would've been better,

If that artist wouldn't have been destroyed,

Maybe his life would've been more peaceful,

If that puppy wouldn't have been hit,

At least someone would've been able to enjoy simple happiness.

I would've wished to tenderly caress those souls,

they were wronged,

I hope God already has.

53

Untamed Cow.

Horns and lights,

So many of these people, but a few bring me a fright,

Yet I walk precipitously and carelessly through these streets,

Sauntering the roads and bridges.

I galloped away from my cattle house,

Abandoning my playmates and family In the ambition of finding leisure,

However here I am in a very bizarre land,

With little to no place to walk or to stand!

I pity these humans who can't find a place to stroll,

Due to their own vehicles,

Even more, those who sit by the sides begging for food and water,

Yet, the irony is,

those children seem happier to me to have found food than the grumpy teenagers riding in the cars,

With all the luxury they could ever please, their fulfilment of happiness still won't appease.

My ears flap high and low,

While my body swishes and sway in the middle of this hustle and chaos,

The trees are visible, but I can't ignore the dirt collected underneath them,

I know he feels suffocated and choked to be harvested above this debris,

Feeling sorry for his condition,

I blink a drop of a tear and walk away,

A bird soars up in the sky,

And while I watch with amusement,

I hear a honk from behind.

Calmly I walk free,

Above the clouds,

Under the sea.

On a road filled with sugar-coated misery,

Calmly I walk free.

54

Embroidery.

You chose the prettiest colours of thread and stitched the white cloth you were given, endeavouring to find the perfect spots to fit in every thread with. The thread was of satin, and each time you found the most perfect point to prick your pin with, you felt like silk, euphoria, more like ecstasy fled through your veins and your blood and you finally found your breath.

You found breath yet still you felt your heart pounding so harshly, almost out of your rib cage in the sense that each time you pricked the perfect spot, you "accidentally" pricked your finger, over and over and over again and now the white cloth was stained with red blood.

Still.

It was the perfection that mattered, the blue thread goes there and no the yellow one absolutely cannot be sown next to the brown one. You started counting the reactions of people when they'd see your embroidery before counting the tears your eyes shed in pain. They didn't even matter to you.

After all, whatever you were creating was still the bare minimum, wasn't it?

You intentionally ignored the worry of people when they told you that there was blood everywhere, you were outrightly bleeding but they all felt like muffled voices in front of the words you wanted to hear so badly.

"You're perfect."

And now the cloth is soaked in blood, your finger, it doesn't hurt,

Apparently, you're invincible.

Each time you say

"I'm fine" to those people whose voices are already muffled in your brain,

You know you mean it more to yourself,

The little hope you have that can finally make you acknowledge the fact that You're not.

One day, the validation won't matter as much. You'll find yourself more important, and realise your worth. One day your heart won't pound as much, your face won't be red, and you'll be calm instead of pretending to be. One day,

"I'm fine" would be an affirmative sentence rather than a persuasive one to your own self,

I promise.

55

Everything Feels So Impassive.

I stare at my silver watch so deeply, so intensely and the minutes just keep passing second by second as if this feeling of numbness would continue contaminating my body till the end of time.

Would it?

How could the clock have the audacity to say it's 7:35 pm already when all my senses have been seized, entirely convinced into believing that it's been 3 am since the past 6 hours?

The passionless restlessness, does it stay? Does it reside eventually in my mind, does it make it its home?

Will I never be able to get up gleefully and enthusiastically, dancing my way into the kitchen, in my room, because all of a sudden I'm at the library curled up like it's the 1st of January and I'm whimpering in the cold,

I guess we ran out of blankets.

And maybe I will just fall asleep if that's how it will continue to feel,

if time continues to be this way.

I almost feel like I'm about to be arrested by time and get locked inside the cage of the clock,

I'll try making friends with the minute hand and the hour hand with the hope that one day I'll convince them to move back a bit, maybe lack a lot of control at that but even if for a millisecond

if I could make the world believe that we're a minute behind,

Maybe I would be able to make myself understand too,

My despaired world too will crumble soon, even if just for a minute.

Let time continue till eternity but maybe I'll be able to stop my world from drowning,

without falling asleep in an attempt of falling into oblivion.

Is it just me?, or am I stuck in an inevitable situation, a circle, a roller coaster ride with no end except I'm on the seat at 3 am, looking at the stars wishfully glaring,

Thinking.

Will I ever be able to reach them?

And it's one of those days, I answer that question with a sigh, an exhaustion in my voice, almost trained to speak

"We will, just not today."

56

High Society.

3 asked 1 how to stay sleek and slender,

1 was greatly handsome,

he whispered "I'm special"

Unknown to the fact that his own ego would later be his doom.

3 wept at his obese shape,

Without realising that the mirror he had befriended was a liar.

2 was the most competitive and cutthroat student to exist,

She was the overachiever, top of her school, little miss perfect.

In reality,

she thought her achievements reflected her self-worth,

No perfectionist she was,

only that wrecked mentality of her made her believe so.

4 was the funny one,

he cracked jokes as a coping mechanism for all the academics he had to deal with,

Being the brother of 2,

He was classified as the smart one before even being born,

Truth be told, he dreaded it,

And so he cracked jokes,

Under panic and anxiety,

But the numbers only laughed and giggled,

No one saw the whimpering boy behind the humorous voice.

6 was 5's sidekick,

5 enjoyed dominating the numbers,

Because she felt that she was the worst,

And so she pretended to be the best,

How typical, you ask of me.

6 was innocent,

All she ever wished for was for everyone to be happy,

But people too kind are taken advantage of,

Her mind was the softest,

and 5 had already claimed her sovereignty over it.

Number 7 was a gentleman,

He was born with charm, yet no one ever noticed,

Because people only judge a person by their looks,

And it was a fact that wasn't even a tiny bit altered in the world of numbers.

8 was the show-off,

But ignorance made him realise he never had a future of his own,

He was so busy living in the present.

9 was arrogant, or as her classmates called her,

Anti-social she was,

But also intelligent,

She never really liked any of the numbers,

Because of how she saw each.

The numbers called her a maniac, a psychopath,

But if you ask me,

She was the most sane of them all.

57

I Love You More on the Days You Don't Feel Like Yourself.

On the days when your morning cup of coffee suddenly tastes too bitter, the songs you played are the ones you don't wanna hear even though you shuffled them in the first place. It's alright, I still love you. I still love you on the days your collar just doesn't perfectly tuck, on the days your school tie just wants to get stuck,

The days you wake up from sleep but your eyes still hurt because you stayed up all night studying but you felt it was the bare minimum anyways. On the days you argue with your teacher because you decided to put your grades above your health once again.

"Kid, this is unhealthy."

"Ma'am, I like to believe I'm invincible"

You brush it off with a joke that's not even funny to yourself now.

On the days you question if anything matters, you question how far you've come, on the days you choose to hug yourself because you're afraid no one will ever offer you one,

It's alright. I'm here for you.

I love you more on the days you try to eat your worries away and then look at yourself with guilt,

"You're still too young to be addicted to caffeine."

(People just like to assume that my blood's composition is more caffeine than haemoglobin at this point.)

It's alright, I love you more on the days when suddenly maths doesn't feel like your best friend, physics looks too foreign for your eyes to understand, chemistry saturates your brain, and you haven't even started biology.

It's okay. It'll pass.

"We need to have a deal, you take care of yourself for me, I take care of myself for you. Please?"

"I promise you. I'll try treating myself with the empathy you give me."

It's okay to feel like you're breaking apart every given second of every single day, I love you more on those days you do because even before glass shatters, it still manages to look so perfectly new.

No one sees your troubles but I do, I love you more on the days that don't make you feel you

Life is but a dream.

Imagine one day you woke up from your sleep, only to findyourself in a completely white, silent, serene and quiet room. There is no source of light from where the bright light is coming, it is just white everywhere. The room is neither cold, nor warm, it is eerily the right temperature. You walk and walk for miles, trying to make sense of what's happening but you can't.

What if life truly were just a dream?

What if reality is really only a simulation?, who knows, one day just an eye twitch can pull that switch holding you back from making all of this a memory. A right memory.

Don't some moments make you gasp in attraction, make your mind abandon all of its sanity and just stare at them forever? Till infinity, and you know it's not possible but the lenses in your eyes cant regain their focus as if some sort of imaginary spell has manipulated them, an attraction, a tiny pebble in the pond of depth, there is so much more to explore in these moments, to count the number of freckles her face, to see how sunlight tiptoes through the broad leaves of the trees in summer afternoons or to simply cherish the way someone smiles. Maybe these moments are the ones that feel so ethereal, you almost feel lustrous, about to fall, and get lost inside the dream till the never ending battery of the clock in the most antique shop stops moving the hour and minute hand.

Grass is always greener on the other side.

Though this saying signifies competitiveness, I believe it has a more beautiful, more incomprehensible meaning.

The grass IS always greener on the other side as it is human tendency to always want more, different, better, to search and to search till the eyes start going shut, till the euphoria finally reaches the senses, till there is a hope of peace in the middle of chaos. Till there is hope.

And, maybe that's just what I believe but,

Have you ever met a person who doesn't have a song they dance their heart to? Like it's their life, have you ever met a reader who doesn't talk about their favourite book as if they get lost in another world when they read it, so much so that when they speak about it, they are still not found. Ever met a poet who ran out rhymes? And letters and sentences and uniquely crafted words?

It is escapism, the grass is not always greener on the other side, the grass is something entirely apart,

Something divinely attractive on the other side.

The End.

www.ingramcontent.com/pod-product-compliance
Lightning Source LLC
LaVergne TN
LVHW041101150826
845673LV00007B/1878